This Night, Hold Me Close:

23 Psalms

poems by

Richard Edgar Wilson

Finishing Line Press
Georgetown, Kentucky

This Night, Hold Me Close:

23 Psalms

"In the old way of saying it, tales were spun; they were threads that tied things together and from them the fabric of the world was woven. In the strongest stories we see ourselves, connected to one another, woven into the pattern, see that we ourselves are stories, telling and being told. Stories like yours and worse than yours are all around, and your suffering won't mark you out as special, though your response to it might."
—from The Faraway Nearby, *Rebecca Solnit*

"We keep making poetry because we are ourselves poems."
—*Abram Van Engen*

ACKNOWLEDGMENTS

I want to express my most sincere appreciation for my wonderful mentors
and instructors from the Austin Stone Institute: Lindsay Funkhouser,
Erin Beasley, and Brian Lundin. I'm grateful for all of the critiques and edits
and, most notably, encouragement over the years. And to the best writing
partner I have ever had, Daniel: this would not have happened without you.
Thanks to all.

Publisher: Leah Huete de Maines
Editor: Christen Kincaid
Cover Art: Richard Edgar Wilson
Author Photo: Richard Edgar Wilson
Cover Design: Elizabeth Maines McCleavy

Order online: www.finishinglinepress.com
also available on amazon.com

Author inquiries and mail orders:
Finishing Line Press
PO Box 1626
Georgetown, Kentucky 40324
USA

Contents

Invocation

Unknown Things

How strange to the sense
      this disjoint organism   its devotion
      to designs and desires   small
shocks of impulse

Someday you must tell me
      why when i am afraid   i slam
      shut my eyes   when fearful
      i am also   of the dark   of the
unknown things

I must hear more of
      why wild warmth
      with its activations its activities   instead of
      the stolid stasis of cold   is
the body's comfort

I must learn why i look
      to the stars   those monuments
      to distance and memory
to mystery
for guidance

And i must know
      since i seek silence for my solace
what it means that when i am sad
i sing

**part one
this night**

Song for City Sunset

This lonely, violent place;

its sounds:
bittersweet brew
stalking steel wolf snarling
somewhere in
unseen pathways nearby,
and the charming chirp of carefree
birds, who cant avian arias, maybe
in innocence, in ignorance. Maybe its
nothing. But
I believe they
know, they note:
whistling in bold defiance of
the hubris hubbub of the
predator, chuckling conspiratorially
because no bully of a car can yet
fly, and reach them.
they can still
elude, escape,
in tree, on rooftop,
lofting, lifting, laughing into
the very cloud
and wind.

not audible over
roaring rubber
on rubbly road
the Grasses grow
resilient, resolute in
restoration. consolation patches
hum together hushed
hymns, as a whisperwind sounds their crevices.
all as one they craft
a supple song, soft,

serene. Once, as a child, you saw a
someone, a senior, a simpleton, a
saint—pluck just the right
Blade, slaughtering it, slivering it,
but also

holding it
just so

tenderly, delicately, breathing
upon it and into it.
It sings in delight,
glorious, giddy as a giggly girl, a
Hallelujah
peculiar and unique
unto itself.

eventually
the Vehicle, as they all do,
all will,
vanishes, vacates, no more violates

This lovely, violet place.

Waxing Crescent, January 6

Some would say she is a smile,
Rising,
welcoming us to a new era;
or a mirror carefully curved,
reflecting back to us
our image just as we desire
to see it.

No, say others: she is a bowl,
Empty,
crafted to catch celestial tears;
or she is the wicked
glistening end of a new sickle,
eager to cut down ripe
golden life.

Everything I Need to Know I Learned from a Meme

Images, wrenched from their rightful place,
a place unknown to us (taken without license)
& cut, cropped, slashed;
forced to serve their new masters to advance causes
that are not their own—

Now: branded with words inflexible as
antiquated laws (shotgun weddings of wisdom)
& stained with font that is
imposing, obtrusive, obscurant,
and unapologetically White.

Bodies

1   This Body of Work

we love our
round numbers. praise them.
applaud them.
ten years. a hundred this or thats.
a billion whatevers.
etcetera.
someone give me a goddam
award then.
zero is as round as it gets.
as round as

2   This Body of Death

the usurping moon.
halflight hack, bastard
brother. faithless, fatherless
f__k. its sporadic appearances,
the hapless jackass that shows up
only to borrow, never to repay.
Its onesided friendship,
beckoning, luring us, promising to siren
the way to some sacred silver when
all it shows us is
the way to itself. It is
its own end.

F__k its seductive pluck
of our waters, like it has
any business at all exerting a
force on us, drinking our wine and
leaving us with just the hangover.
Its allure is only
a mirage. It has

nothing to offer but
dust. Craters and darkness and
dust.
The same for
the stars. Their lust is simply to
burn; to consume, take up space;
their sole desire to attract, to
outshine; to be seen and known like a
mansplain, a cosmic
condescension begging to be
validated and recognized and
remembered.

Meanwhile they
torch everything that makes them
what they are until they
collapse and take
the whole universe down
into inescapable black
with them. F__k

the lie that is
the night.

———

Tomorrow will be
one hundred degrees
and at least the Sun,
though i am scorched,
killed,

is honest.

3   *Andromeda*

the next nearest source of light
is still so far away
that no matter how much closer it is
than all the others
it is still
just a tiny unreachable thing
it looks
no different
indifferent
to a desperate people
searching the obsidian sky

: for light

the sun
is all we have)

Now I lay me down to sleep

Now I lay me down to sleep
To let eyes close instead of weep.
But tragedy is lodged so deep
That even while I'm counting sheep,
Yes, even when I am asleep,
Still hissing snakey sorrows seep.

Now I lay me down to rest.
Is this creation's awful jest?
Or just some strange endurance test?
That bodies, even at their best,
Must every day return to nest
To flee the mourning in their breast.

Now I lay me down this night,
So hold me close; oh, hold me tight.
For if it is to be my plight
(Although it gives me deathly fright)
Not to see tomorrow's light:
Well this, I think, would be alright.

A Break

thanks to technology we
can now measure ourselves
even while asleep as if
it were not enough to
quantify everything else all day.
speed limits, meeting times, calls,
dollars, cents, pounds, miles. starts &
stops.

quality. quantity. breath.
heart rate. hours of REM, deep, wake.
my wearable monitors my movements
and minutes and sorts them
as a coin counter does
loose change. in the morning i get
a score between a hundred &
zero.

occasionally it's in the nineties, if i check
all the right boxes, the length and depth and
appropriateness of it all. a hundred is
not possible, i am told. i wonder, though
what depths of rest i might achieve
if i were to lie perfectly still, my heart rate
at zero, the hours both infinite &
finished.

after all,
what is it to be tired
except the need to always
count

here and now

a free app on my phone promises me
a map of this night sky
which makes no sense from here
i mean this here,
which doesn't really
mean anything because
here is merely a now,
only a small now, a right now,
and your now is not even my now
and our now is not a now for them
but a then
what is this here this
right now that makes it
the right now?
from there from then we might be
certainly are
invisible.

a map of the universe
from here is only
a shitty record of all the things that
used to be all the things that
are no longer true or
alive. but if we could
see them not as they were but
as they now are—
the true now the one now—
is this the same
as seeing our own future?
now that's an app i'd pay for
as long as there was
anything
to see—

time, distance, wisdom

because the stars(
crisply dotting darkened drape of night
moses miniatures mapping routes to glory
telling fates and fortunes
poking pleasure specks into my eyes, when else is black
shaping wings ,claws ,arrows
    faces fantastic
)aren't truly stars at all
      but factories of fury
      incomprehensible fountains ,fires
and at the very least
    are grossly, utterly
          unreachable
    in this lifetime, any
      racing further away
        each minute, second, nano
and very well might be
    by now
    simmered out
      shattered in sparks and fire and
        ravenous ravaging molecule bursts
        left:
            sucking husks
            gravity wells
    dark and void
      selfish and
          soundless
but here
        from my tiny hurtling perch
    they are
bright and small and
beautiful

Amon-Ra

the particular, peculiar
purple of dusk
lies not in the light fleeing us,
but rather in whole hosts
of persons, we, turning, in concert,
daily away from
it.

(and darkness, as we know,
is the time for secrets, for shame,
for solitude and deadly deeds, for
theft, for stealth, for
private weeping, for
lonely bedtime
sorrows.)

the blessed, bashful
blush of dawn
is that of embarrassed gratitude
that when we have turned 'round again
sol's sharp shards are still there to reveal us,
at least for one more
day.

Psalm for Daybreak

Unabashed
        cleaner than its end,
        which whimpered in bruised hues
        offering a prismatic
        apology for shortcomings, missteps,
        miseries & slinking coyly off
        the stage
        to let other suns
        sing their bit parts
        for an interlude

Unrivaled
        prouder than its exit
        the show's star returns
        begins blazing orange the east,
        a wildfire uncontained, spreading
        slowly, steadily & banishing
        all trace
        of incoherent indigo
        and no other light
        can share in its aria aura

Unyielding
        the expanse once
        impenetrable onyx
        now shouts alive with
        baby blue, that of clear waters
        of joyous proclamations &
        the arrival
        of newest life, like the
        announcement that soon,
        a Son will be born.

**part two
hold me**

driving in the dark early one morning

The streets creak reluctantly awake.
Scurrying hurrying by go the vehicles of
salesmen and bankers, movers, shakers, makers of things, their
headlights stabbing yellow knives into the sleeping flesh of
night, shuddering merciless into the still rumble
waves of engine growl. These are the
drivers of cars and economies, every effort matters, every
pedal pushed, gas or brake, timing is everything, and everyone
hurtles along
together foreignly fast, envelopes already pushing, shoving, as if
today only existed to atone for
what was forgotten yesterday.

Sidelined and
sitting passive,
watching waning peaceful dark,
my car is parked and
silent, still dewed from evening rain and i
wonder how i might politely, gently, undisturbedly
decline to drive anywhere this day.

When We Talked about Children

It's late when I call
from my hotel room. We are
in different time zones, but
you are still up. I'm glad. I ask how you are.
Fine, you say. We make small talk
for a while. You tell me about your day.
Uneventful. I tell you about mine.
It wasn't much
different.

Then I ask about
our children. They're sleeping,
you tell me, with a tone that says
that should have been obvious.
I ask if you can wake them up.
I'd love to talk to them. I miss them.
Seems like I haven't seen them
in a long time. Maybe
forever.

I don't think so, you say. It's
far too late for that.
Of course, I say. I get it.
I should have asked
earlier, when this day
was younger, before the
sun had set on you. You say
nothing, which says
everything.

To You, In Late Autumn

Our roses have begun to wilt,
collapsing, covering their hearts,
weary of seeding other life,
now all they want to do is sleep.
Our tiny field once springy green
now hunkers down, tired and brown.
It crunches under leaden foot,
leaving a space for winter weeds

which will grow unruly, unchecked
until our sore hands uproot them
one more time, like in seasons past.
Then come next spring we'll plant again.
But this can only happen if
we can outwait the coming winds
that dry and split and freeze and kill
whatever they happen to touch.

The frost will pass, and warmth return,
with enough time. It always does.
But maybe we are out of time.

Maybe the spring will not return
and we have already wasted
our precious few allotted days

and all that's left for us is cold.
Quite possibly we'll starve before
our garden blooms again next year—

or maybe the one after that,
if we, if you, can wait that long.

Gödel to his beloved

my interest in you is the
lock's interest in the key,
as breaking like robin's eggs your
carefullest hands break me apart birthing
new mes, new keys in new doors which
open onto spring and green things. it is the
eye's interest in the photon, off all things bounce
pieces flecks of what i can only say is you, all songs sing
notes whose meter is onliest you. it is the
wire's interest in the current, ancient strings copperly
stretched through prisoning planks, passive and cold,
waiting for the spark. it is the
page's flaccid fragile interest in the pen, flat, inert,
madly hoping blank and emptier than
holes, white and still and
wordless.

Sonnets: A Sonnet

A sonnet is an antiquated form,
a structure now in use by very few.
In centuries gone by it was the norm
when it was revolutionary, new.
The lovestruck poet would attempt to mold
his ardent words into this certain shape,
and hope perchance his lover would behold
his efforts, and would stand entranced, agape.
But if I were to write a sonnet now,
and hope that with its gift I would impress,
no doubt she would at best just wonder how
this backwards idiot could even dress.
Yet this is all I know, my only skill:
Anachronistic words, inert and still.

Audrey : Three haiku

I

We enter a last
building, our dog beside us.
We'll leave without her.

II

"She still looks like a
puppy," the vet says. "Yes," I
say, "She always has."

III

Afterwards we go
to our usual haunt. We
see some friends. It helps

a little.

**part three
close**

bold as love

1   the show

the picture is old
and grainy, foggy like
rainy, murky like
muddy streams, algae,
sloth, & resignation

a bluish blush from
humbly underneath
purple headband a
smoky synesthesia haze
green & new

while the wind cries
sad you summon her
she comes to you winging,
little your voice blooms
songs 4 mourning

and now the sound
shears redapplecrisp and
stratosphereclear, bright with
tones, twangs, trainy
thumps & glides

and hums. fingers rumble
along railway struts, strings—
fast, nimble, urgent like
an ambulance axis:
lives @ stake

it is foxy enough
to henhouse my breath
just for an instant
which is almost unnoticeable,
gentle & ladylike

epiphony through an amplifier:
respiration is less essential
than this sudden ancient must
to be electrically (as you are)
1 with something—

anything, something as
bold as perhaps black cups
of joe, shot through with
zebra milky joy. something as bold
as (please) love .

fine

2 encore

now the gray cloud
clears tangerinefresh and
airnear, bright with
synthesis days
green & new

while the wind dies
merry i summon you
you come to me singing,
large your voice booms
songs 4 peace.

take anything you want
from me; for i
was
yellow &
black & blue

selah

A Stage, At a Festival

Someone designs
These Lights:
their lives, their infinite imminent Cycles,
their flashes of blue, blasts of bleedy red, bursts of growy
green, the Green unSeen, the
penetrating shouts of crystal white,
rainbow hands clapping to fever beats, thrashing thumps,
Dissonant chords, soothing strums,
nimble, patient melodies,
Weary, teary trumpets sending us to
A Final Fade away.

The Designer
Knows
how Light
Changes us, how it
Makes us into or out of something, how it
Moves us and turns us and
Enters us, becomes part of us and
Is us, or was us
Once,
before it became
Light.

As we will too
in due time,
Our particles fleeing apart
scattering like seed back out into
Earth—this Earth,
Other Earths,
Other Beings
Other Life.

We don't actually see anything.
That tree, that car,

That house, that river,
That rubbish on the street,
That body in the alley.
These hands, these sheets,
This lover in my bed beside me—
These cannot be seen. They may
perhaps be touched, but all that can be seen is
Light, Reflected.

alphabetized inventory of things i apparently care about, based on the contents of my office (non-comprehensive)

baseball
beards
books
books about loss
books about love
books about outer space
books about the inexorability of time
books by famous authors
books by nobodies
comedy
drama
games of various types
half-filled notebooks collecting dust
masterpieces
one hit wonders
poetry
science fiction
stargazing
theology
wanting
wondering
yesterdays
Zion

Copernicus, Oceanus Procellarum (or, Earthrise)

It is no small thing that somehow
in this supposedly advanced age
there are still those who think
the earth is flat when it is
clearly
a sphere. There is no
other side of the world. Only the long slow
curve of an object with
just one side,
in three dimensions.

Or four, if you count time, that fuzz
through which our globe slowly spins,
giving us the impression that
dark is somehow
distinct
from light. There is no
night and day. Only the long broad
sweep of our motion through
common hours,
moving in one direction.

Yogi

I
supine
my heart is suspended in
water, blood, in
flesh,
somewhere between the
hard earth and
heaven

II
the places where i
most ache, burn, are
where i most need to stretch,
engage.
rigor mortis stiff,
avoidance is simply delayed
death.

III
my breath is
yours, and yours mine, as
together all of us counting
inspire,
and wait; hold. then
we together, focused,
expire.

IV
as we depart,
sore and weary, our time
now finished, music sings us,
harps
cascading rising arpeggi pluck
us back to our true
life.

Benediction

Up

A Psalm for Ascension Day

Why
ascend to the sky? Why not just suddenly
disappear, as you had appeared sometimes, in
the upper room or the Emmaus road?
Why the need for
up
at all, for Ascension into
a bright maybe blue expanse, like you were
shattering a low blue ceiling or hammering through
the lid on a jar and flying
up
and off, a butterfly escaping a clumsy prison made by
cruel, weak hands?
                              Unless this up, like
everything you did, was a grace, unless it was
an example, a symbol of some inconceivable
up
wards freedom that we could not
otherwise imagine, any more than our now
rockmodern minds can picture
tongues of Spirit flame, hovering, licking
up
our incomprehension, our inadequacies, our
indifference, our intransigence, our
inability to do anything but
stand around gazing
up
into the sky wondering
where you went, and
when you will return—
                              Unless you
wanted to lift our chins, draw our eyes
up
away from tombs, away from
the dust of shame on our feet, away from
personal Israels that claim our
hearts' thrones and demand our loyalty—

up
to those you picked to stand beside us,
to the green hills you sprinkled with olive trees,
to the delicate heavens you draped above,
to the bright fire of your provision,
to wonder, to awe, to
You.